QUEENSTOWN

Queenstown
Otago, New Zealand

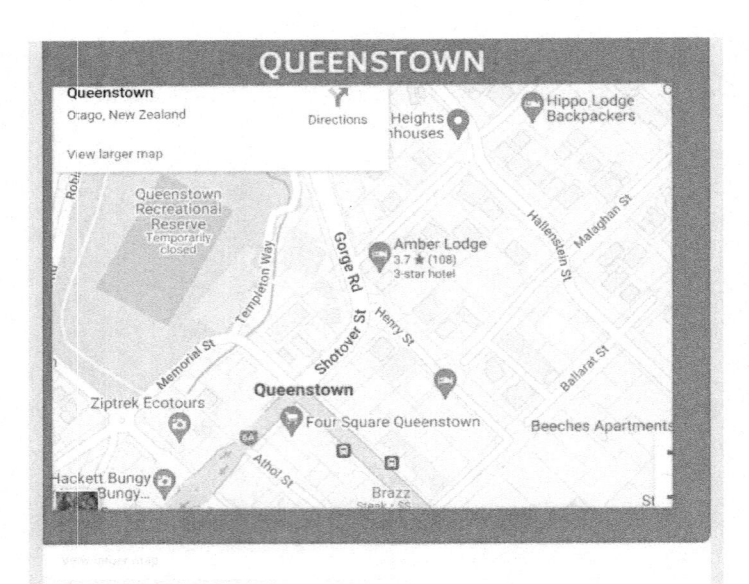

View larger map

SCAN HERE

1. Open the Camera App
2. Select the Rear Camera
3. Point the Camera at the QR Code
4. Align the QR Code with the Camera Frame
5. Tap the Screen to Scan

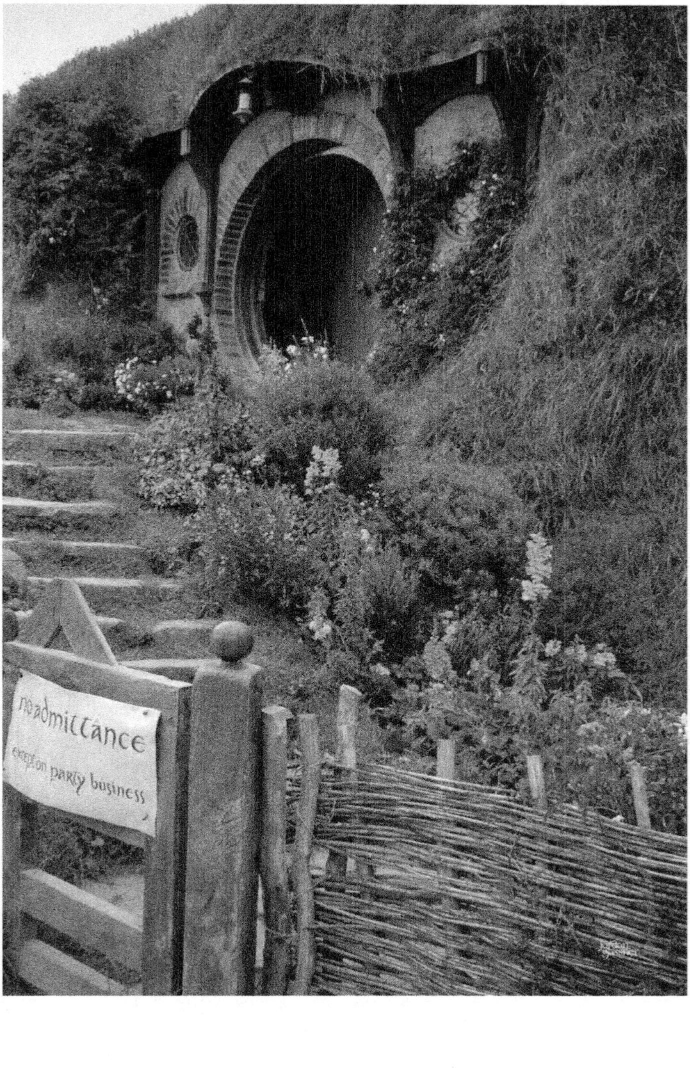
no admittance
except on party business

Chapter 1. Introduction

Welcome to Queenstown

Nestled in the heart of New Zealand's South Island, Queenstown is a gem that attracts visitors from all corners of the globe. Renowned for its stunning natural beauty, adventure sports, and vibrant culture, Queenstown offers an unforgettable experience for every traveller. With the majestic Remarkables mountain range and the serene Lake Wakatipu as its backdrop, Queenstown seamlessly blends outdoor excitement with luxurious comfort and local charm. Whether you're an adrenaline junkie, a nature lover, a foodie, or simply looking to unwind, Queenstown promises a diverse range of activities and sights that cater to all interests.

Why Visit Queenstown in 2024

Unmatched Natural Beauty

In 2024, Queenstown is more enchanting than ever. The region's landscapes, often described as some of the most beautiful in the world, are at their most pristine. The Southern

Alps provide a dramatic skyline, while Lake Wakatipu reflects the surrounding peaks, creating picture-perfect vistas that seem almost unreal. Each season brings its unique charm – from the lush greenery of summer and the fiery autumnal hues to the snowy wonderland of winter and the blossoming vitality of spring.

Thrilling Adventures

Queenstown is often called the "Adventure Capital of the World" and for good reason. The town is a hub for extreme sports and outdoor activities. In 2024, new and improved facilities and experiences await, from bungee jumping off historic bridges and skydiving over breathtaking landscapes to white-water rafting and jet boating in crystal-clear rivers. The ski season is particularly noteworthy this year, with state-of-the-art lifts and expanded terrain at popular resorts like The Remarkables and Coronet Peak, promising an unparalleled experience for skiers and snowboarders of all levels.

Vibrant Culture and Cuisine

Beyond the natural allure and thrill-seeking opportunities, Queenstown boasts a rich cultural scene. The town's calendar in 2024 is packed with events, festivals, and exhibitions celebrating everything from music and art to food and wine. Culinary enthusiasts will find Queenstown a delightful destination, with a burgeoning food scene that emphasizes local produce, innovative cuisine, and world-class wines from the nearby Central Otago wine region. This year, several new restaurants and bars have opened, adding fresh flavours and exciting dining experiences to the already impressive culinary landscape.

Sustainable Tourism Initiatives

Queenstown has made significant strides in sustainable tourism, making 2024 an excellent time to visit for eco-conscious travellers. The town and its businesses have implemented various green initiatives, focusing on conservation and responsible tourism. From eco-friendly accommodations and tours to conservation projects that visitors can participate in, Queenstown is dedicated to preserving its natural beauty for future generations.

Wellness and Relaxation

For those looking to unwind and rejuvenate, Queenstown in 2024 offers an array of wellness retreats and luxury spas. The region's serene environment provides the perfect setting for relaxation and mindfulness. Many resorts and spas have enhanced their wellness programs, incorporating holistic treatments, yoga, meditation, and outdoor wellness activities like forest bathing and guided nature walks.

Unique Local Experiences

This year, Queenstown has introduced more opportunities to connect with the local Maori culture and traditions. Guided tours and cultural experiences are available, offering insights into the rich history and heritage of the indigenous people. These authentic interactions provide a deeper understanding of the region's cultural fabric and enrich the overall travel experience.

How to Use This Guide

Welcome to the ultimate guide to Queenstown in 2024! This comprehensive guide is designed to help you make the most of your visit, whether you're planning a brief stay or an extended adventure. We've organized the information into clear, easy-to-navigate sections, so you can quickly find what you're looking for and tailor your trip to your specific interests and needs.

Sections Overview

1. Getting There and Around Details on how to reach Queenstown and the best ways to navigate the town and its surroundings once you arrive. We cover everything from flights and car rentals to public transport and scenic routes.

2. Accommodation: A curated selection of accommodation options to suit every budget and preference. Whether you're looking for luxury hotels, budget-friendly hostels, family accommodations, or unique stays, we've got you covered.

3. Top Attractions: Must-see sights and experiences that should be on every visitor's list. From iconic landmarks and natural wonders to cultural hotspots and hidden gems, this section highlights the best of Queenstown.

4. Outdoor Activities and Adventure Sports: A detailed look at the outdoor and adventure activities that Queenstown is famous for. This includes everything from hiking and biking to skiing and extreme sports.

5. Food and Drink: Recommendations for the best places to eat and drink in Queenstown. Discover top restaurants, cosy cafes, vibrant bars, and local specialities that you won't want to miss.

6. Shopping: A guide to Queenstown's shopping scene, featuring local boutiques, souvenir shops, and markets where you can find unique gifts and products.

7. Day Trips and Excursions: Ideas for day trips and excursions to explore the surrounding region. Whether you're interested in nearby towns, scenic drives, or nature reserves, this section offers plenty of inspiration.

8. Cultural Experiences: Insights into Queenstown's cultural offerings, including museums, galleries, performances, and opportunities to engage with local Maori culture.

9. Seasonal Highlights: Information on what to expect in each season, including weather, special events, and seasonal activities, helping you plan your trip according to your preferences.

10. Family-Friendly Activities: Suggestions for activities and attractions that are perfect for families travelling with children, ensuring a fun and memorable trip for visitors of all ages.

11. Wellness and Relaxation: Recommendations for spas, wellness retreats, and relaxation activities to help you unwind and rejuvenate during your stay.

12. Nightlife and Entertainment: A guide to Queenstown's nightlife and entertainment options, from bars and nightclubs to live music venues and casinos.

How to Navigate This Guide

Each section of this guide is designed to be standalone, so you can jump directly to the parts that interest you the most. However, for the best experience, we recommend starting with the "Getting There and Around" section if you're in the planning stages of your trip, followed by the "Accommodation" section to choose where you'll stay. Once those basics are covered, explore the "Top Attractions" and "Outdoor Activities" sections to start building your itinerary.

Using the Guide on the Go

This guide is also mobile-friendly, so you can easily access it on your smartphone or tablet while travelling. Bookmark the sections that are most relevant to you and use the guide as a handy reference tool throughout your trip. Each section is filled with practical tips, local insights, and recommendations to help you navigate Queenstown like a pro.

Insider Tips and Local Secrets

Throughout the guide, you'll find insider tips and local secrets highlighted in special boxes. These nuggets of information are designed to give you a deeper, more authentic experience, from the best times to visit popular attractions to hidden spots that locals love.

Practical Information

We've included a practical information section at the end of the guide with essential details like emergency numbers, health and safety tips, currency and banking information, and communication options. This section ensures you have all the necessary information at your fingertips for a smooth and worry-free trip.

Updates and Contact Information

Queenstown is a dynamic destination, and things can change rapidly. We recommend checking the latest information on specific attractions and services before you go. If you have any questions or need additional advice, local visitor centres and tourist information offices in Queenstown are excellent resources.

In conclusion, this guide aims to provide a comprehensive, engaging, and practical resource for planning your trip to Queenstown in 2024. With its stunning natural landscapes, thrilling adventures, rich cultural experiences, and welcoming atmosphere, Queenstown promises a memorable and enriching travel experience. Whether you're a first-time visitor or returning for another adventure, we hope this guide helps you make the most of your time in this extraordinary part of the world. Enjoy your journey, and welcome to Queenstown!

Chapter 2. Getting There

By Air

Queenstown is a popular destination that's accessible by various modes of transportation. The fastest and most convenient way to reach this beautiful town is by air.

Queenstown Airport (ZQN) is located in Frankton, about a 15-minute drive from the town centre. This airport handles both domestic and international flights, making it a key gateway to the Southern Lakes region.

Domestic Flights

Several airlines operate daily flights to Queenstown from major New Zealand cities. Air New Zealand, Jetstar, and Qantas provide frequent services from Auckland, Wellington, and Christchurch. These flights are relatively short, with durations ranging from one to two hours. Domestic flights are often the preferred choice for travellers looking to maximize their time in Queenstown.

International Flights

Queenstown Airport also caters to international travellers with direct flights from Australia. Airlines such as Air New Zealand, Qantas, Jetstar, and Virgin Australia offer services from Sydney, Melbourne, Brisbane, and the Gold Coast. These flights take approximately three to four hours, making Queenstown easily accessible from across the Tasman Sea.

Airport Facilities and Services

Queenstown Airport is well-equipped to handle the influx of visitors. The airport features a variety of amenities to ensure a comfortable and convenient experience. Passengers can enjoy duty-free shopping, dining options, and car rental services within the terminal. The airport also offers free Wi-Fi, currency exchange, and information desks to assist travellers with their queries.

Getting from the Airport to Queenstown

Once you've landed at Queenstown Airport, there are several options to get to the town centre. Taxis and ride-sharing services like Uber are readily available and provide a quick and hassle-free transfer to your accommodation. For those looking to start their adventure immediately, car rental agencies are located at the airport, offering a range of vehicles to suit your needs. Additionally, the Connectabus service provides regular shuttle buses that operate between the airport and the town centre, with tickets available for purchase at the airport or online.

By Road

For those who prefer a scenic journey, travelling to Queenstown by road is an excellent option. The drive to Queenstown offers stunning views of New Zealand's diverse landscapes, from rolling farmlands and majestic mountains to crystal-clear lakes and lush forests.

From Christchurch

The drive from Christchurch to Queenstown is approximately 480 kilometres and takes around six hours. This route, known as State Highway 8, takes you through the Canterbury Plains, the picturesque town of Geraldine, and the stunning Mackenzie Basin, where you'll pass Lake Tekapo and Lake Pukaki. The journey continues through the Lindis Pass, offering breathtaking alpine scenery before reaching Queenstown.

From Dunedin

Travelling from Dunedin to Queenstown is another popular route, covering about 280 kilometres and taking around three and a half hours. The journey follows State Highway 1 and State Highway 8, passing through the historic gold-mining town of Lawrence and the charming town of Alexandra in the Central Otago region. The drive offers diverse landscapes, including vineyards, orchards, and mountain ranges.

From the West Coast

If you're coming from the West Coast, the journey to Queenstown takes you through some of New Zealand's most rugged and dramatic scenery. The drive from Greymouth or Hokitika is approximately 450 kilometres and takes about six hours. This route, following State Highway 6, winds through dense rainforests, over mountain passes, and along the shores of Lake Hawea and Lake Wanaka before reaching Queenstown.

Scenic Stops Along the Way

Whichever route you choose, there are plenty of scenic stops to enjoy along the way. Take your time to explore the charming towns, natural attractions, and lookout points that dot the landscape. Popular stops include the Church of the Good Shepherd at Lake Tekapo, the historic Kawarau Bridge, and the vibrant town of Wanaka with its famous lakeside tree.

By Bus and Train

Bus Services

Travelling by bus is a cost-effective and comfortable option for reaching Queenstown. Several bus companies operate services to Queenstown from major cities and towns across New Zealand. InterCity and Newmans Coach Lines are two of the most well-known providers, offering regular services from Christchurch, Dunedin, and other destinations.

Buses are equipped with comfortable seating, air conditioning, and restrooms, ensuring a pleasant journey. Some services also offer onboard Wi-Fi and charging points for added convenience. The bus journey to Queenstown provides an opportunity to sit back, relax, and take in the stunning scenery along the way.

Train Services

While Queenstown does not have a direct train service, travellers can combine train and bus travel for a unique and scenic journey. One popular option is the TranzAlpine train, which operates between Christchurch and Greymouth. This journey is often hailed as one of the most beautiful train rides in the world, taking passengers through the majestic Southern Alps, across viaducts, and through lush rainforests.

Upon reaching Greymouth, travellers can then take a bus or drive to Queenstown, enjoying the scenic route through the West Coast and Central Otago regions. While this option takes longer than a direct bus or car journey, it offers a memorable and picturesque way to experience New Zealand's diverse landscapes.

Transportation Tips

Plan Ahead

Whether you're flying, driving, or taking a bus, it's essential to plan your journey. During peak seasons, such as summer and winter holidays, flights and accommodations can fill up quickly. Booking your tickets and accommodations well ahead of time ensures you secure the best options and avoid any last-minute stress.

Car Rentals

If you're planning to explore Queenstown and its surroundings, renting a car provides the freedom and flexibility to travel at your own pace. Several car rental companies operate at Queenstown Airport and in the town centre, offering a range of vehicles to suit different needs and budgets. Make sure to book your rental car in advance, especially during peak seasons, to ensure availability.

Road Conditions and Safety

New Zealand's roads are generally well-maintained, but driving in some areas can be challenging, especially for those unfamiliar with the terrain. In winter, road conditions can be affected by snow and ice, particularly in alpine regions. It's essential to check weather and road conditions before setting out and to carry snow chains if travelling in winter.

Driving in New Zealand is on the left-hand side of the road. Make sure to familiarize yourself with local road rules and signs. Take regular breaks during long drives, and ensure you have sufficient fuel, especially in remote areas where service stations may be scarce.

Public Transportation in Queenstown

Once you arrive in Queenstown, getting around the town is easy and convenient. The town centre is compact and pedestrian-friendly, with many attractions, shops, and restaurants within walking distance. For longer distances or to explore the surrounding areas, several transportation options are available.

Buses and Shuttles

The Orbus service, operated by the Otago Regional Council, provides regular bus services within Queenstown and to nearby areas, including Arrowtown and Frankton. The buses are affordable and convenient, making them an excellent option for getting around town without a car.

In addition to public buses, several shuttle services operate in Queenstown, offering transport to popular attractions, ski fields, and nearby towns. These shuttles are a convenient way to explore the region, especially for those who prefer not to drive.

Taxis and Ride-Sharing

Taxis are readily available in Queenstown, with several companies operating in the area. Taxis can be hailed on the street, booked by phone, or arranged through your accommodation. Ride-sharing services like Uber are also available, providing an alternative to traditional taxis.

Biking and Walking

Queenstown is a bike-friendly town with numerous cycling trails and bike rental shops. Biking is a great way to explore the town and its surroundings, offering a fun and eco-friendly mode of transportation. Many accommodations and activity providers also offer bike hire, making it easy to incorporate cycling into your itinerary.

Walking is another excellent way to get around Queenstown, especially within the town centre. The compact layout and pedestrian-friendly streets make it easy to explore on foot. Several scenic walking trails start from the town centre, offering beautiful views of the lake and mountains.

Parking

If you're driving in Queenstown, it's important to be aware of parking options and regulations. The town centre has several public car parks and metered street parking. Parking can be limited, especially during peak seasons, so it's advisable to arrive early or use public transportation when possible.

Some accommodations offer free or discounted parking for guests, so be sure to check with your hotel or rental property. Pay attention to parking signs and restrictions to avoid fines, and always park in designated areas.

Environmental Considerations

Queenstown is committed to sustainable tourism, and visitors are encouraged to minimize their environmental impact. Consider using public transportation, biking, or walking whenever possible to reduce your carbon footprint. If you're renting a car, opt for a fuel-efficient or hybrid vehicle. Be mindful of waste disposal and recycling, and support local businesses that prioritize sustainability.

Getting to Queenstown is part of the adventure, whether you're soaring over the Southern Alps by air, enjoying a scenic road trip, or taking a comfortable bus journey. Each mode of transportation offers its own unique experiences and advantages, allowing you to choose the option that best suits your preferences and travel style.

By planning and considering the various transportation tips provided, you can ensure a smooth and enjoyable journey to this remarkable destination. Once you arrive, Queenstown's diverse landscapes, thrilling activities, and vibrant culture await, promising an unforgettable experience in one of the world's most beautiful locations.

Chapter 3. Accommodation

When planning your stay in Queenstown, you'll find a wide range of accommodation options to suit every budget, preference, and travel style. From luxurious hotels and boutique lodges to budget-friendly hostels and unique stays, Queenstown offers something for everyone. Let's explore the various types of accommodation available in this charming town.

Luxury Hotels

For travellers seeking indulgence and pampering, Queenstown boasts a selection of luxurious hotels that promise unparalleled comfort and opulence.

1. Eichardt's Private Hotel

Located on the shores of Lake Wakatipu in the heart of Queenstown, Eichardt's Private Hotel is a historic icon renowned for its elegance and sophistication. Offering stunning lake and mountain views, this boutique hotel features beautifully appointed suites and apartments, each exuding charm and character. Guests can enjoy personalized service, fine dining at The Grille by Eichardt's, and access to exclusive amenities such as a private spa and concierge services.

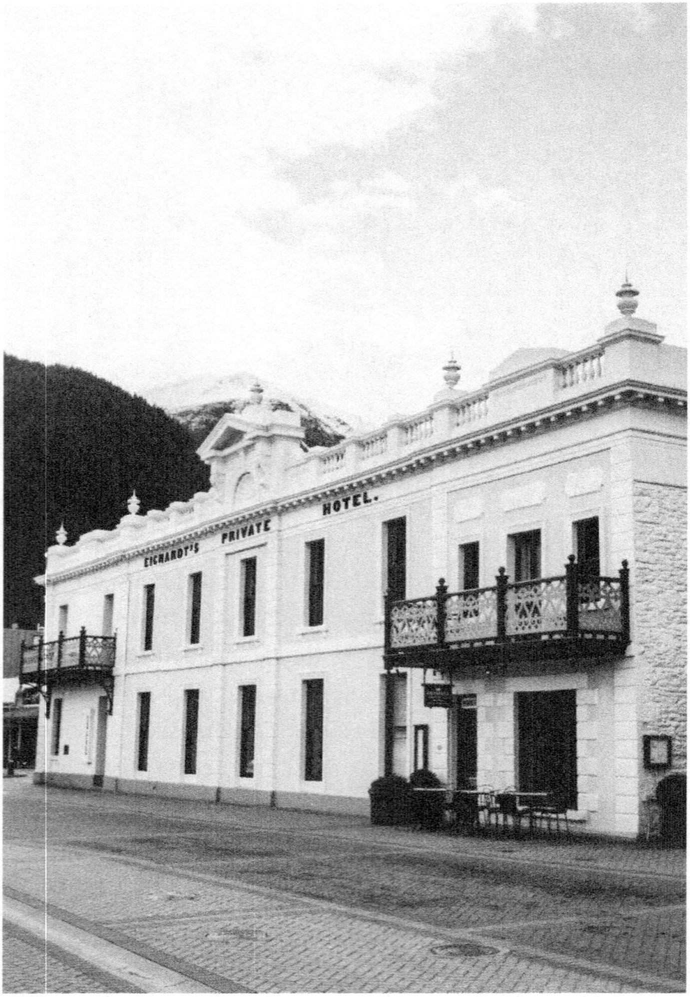
EICHARDT'S PRIVATE HOTEL.

2. Matakauri Lodge

Nestled on the shores of Lake Wakatipu, Matakauri Lodge is a luxurious retreat that combines contemporary design with breathtaking natural beauty. The lodge offers spacious suites and villas with panoramic views of the lake and mountains, as well as world-class amenities including a spa, infinity pool, and gourmet restaurant. With its serene setting and attentive staff, Matakauri Lodge provides a tranquil escape for discerning travellers.

3. The Rees Hotel & Luxury Apartments

Situated on the edge of Lake Wakatipu, The Rees Hotel & Luxury Apartments offers five-star accommodation with a focus on comfort and elegance. The hotel features spacious rooms and suites, many of which offer stunning lake and mountain views. Guests can indulge in gourmet dining at True South Dining Room, relax at the on-site spa, or take advantage of the hotel's complimentary shuttle service to explore Queenstown's attractions.

Budget-Friendly Options

Budget travel doesn't have to mean compromising on convenience or comfort. Queenstown offers a variety of affordable accommodation options that cater to budget-conscious travellers.

1. YHA Queenstown Central

Located in the heart of Queenstown, YHA Queenstown Central is a popular choice for budget travellers seeking affordable and comfortable accommodation. The hostel offers a range of dormitory-style and private rooms, as well as communal facilities such as a fully equipped kitchen, lounge area, and outdoor courtyard. With its central location and friendly atmosphere, YHA Queenstown Central provides a convenient base for exploring the town and its surroundings.

2. Nomads Queenstown Backpackers

Situated just a short walk from the town centre, Nomads Queenstown Backpackers offers budget-friendly accommodation with a vibrant and social atmosphere. The hostel features dormitory-style and private rooms, as well as communal areas including a shared kitchen, lounge, and outdoor patio. Guests can also enjoy the hostel's on-site bar and restaurant, which hosts regular events and activities for guests to socialize and meet fellow travellers.

3. JUCY Snooze Queenstown

JUCY Snooze Queenstown offers affordable and stylish accommodations for budget travellers, with a range of dormitory-style and private rooms available. The hostel features modern facilities and amenities, including a communal kitchen, lounge area, and outdoor courtyard. Guests can also take advantage of the hostel's convenient location, just a short walk from Queenstown's attractions, shops, and restaurants.

Family-Friendly Stays

Traveling with family requires accommodation that caters to the needs of both adults and children. Queenstown offers a variety of family-friendly stays that provide comfort, convenience, and entertainment for guests of all ages.

1. Novotel Queenstown Lakeside

Situated on the shores of Lake Wakatipu, Novotel Queenstown Lakeside is a family-friendly hotel that offers spacious rooms and suites with stunning lake and mountain views. The hotel features a range of amenities for families, including an indoor pool, hot tub, and children's play area. Families can also enjoy dining at the on-site restaurant, which offers a kids' menu and special family packages.

2. Copthorne Hotel & Apartments Queenstown Lakeview

Located within walking distance of the town centre, Copthorne Hotel & Apartments Queenstown Lakeview offers comfortable accommodations with spectacular lake and mountain views. The hotel features family-friendly apartments with separate bedrooms and living areas, as well as a range of amenities including an outdoor pool, spa, and playground. Families can also take advantage of the hotel's babysitting services and children's activities, ensuring a fun and relaxing stay for all.

3. Oaks Queenstown Club Suites

Oaks Queenstown Club Suites is an apartment-style hotel that offers spacious and fully equipped accommodations suitable for families. The hotel features one-, two-, and three-bedroom apartments with modern amenities, including full kitchens, laundry facilities, and separate living areas. Families can also enjoy the hotel's outdoor heated pool, barbecue area, and children's playground, as well as its convenient location just a short drive from Queenstown's attractions and activities.

Unique Accommodations

For travellers seeking a one-of-a-kind experience, Queenstown offers a variety of unique accommodations that promise unforgettable memories and moments of wonder.

1. Azur Lodge

Perched on a hillside overlooking Lake Wakatipu and the Remarkables mountain range, Azur Lodge offers luxury villas with stunning panoramic views. Each villa features floor-to-ceiling windows, a private terrace, and a cosy fireplace, creating a serene and intimate retreat. Guests can also enjoy personalized service, gourmet dining, and a range of activities, including helicopter tours and wine-tasting experiences.

2. The Green Kiwi Backpacker Hostel

For a quirky and eco-friendly stay, The Green Kiwi Backpacker Hostel offers unique accommodations in a converted train carriage. Located just a short drive from Queenstown, this eco-hostel features dormitory-style rooms and communal facilities including a shared kitchen, lounge, and outdoor patio. Guests can also explore the surrounding area, which includes walking trails, a river, and native bushland.

3. Hilton Queenstown Resort & Spa

Set on the shores of Lake Wakatipu, Hilton Queenstown Resort & Spa offers luxurious accommodations in a stunning alpine setting. The hotel features a range of unique accommodations, including spacious suites, lakefront villas, and cosy cabins. Guests can enjoy world-class amenities, including a day spa, heated indoor pool, and multiple dining options. The hotel also offers a range of activities, from kayaking and fishing to golf and snow sports, ensuring an unforgettable stay for guests of all ages.

Whether you're seeking luxury and indulgence, travelling on a budget, vacationing with family, or looking for a unique experience, Queenstown has the perfect accommodation for you. From luxurious hotels and budget-friendly hostels to family-friendly stays and unique lodgings, Queenstown offers a diverse range of options to suit every traveller's needs and preferences. Whatever your choice, you're sure to find comfort, convenience, and hospitality in this charming town nestled amidst New Zealand's stunning landscapes.

Chapter 4. Getting Around

Exploring Queenstown and its surrounding areas is a breeze thanks to its efficient transportation options. Whether you prefer the convenience of public transport, the flexibility of renting a car, the freedom of cycling and walking, or the ease of taxi and ride-sharing services, Queenstown offers something for every traveller.

Public Transport

1. Orbus

Orbus is Queenstown's public bus service, operated by the Otago Regional Council. It provides an affordable and convenient way to get around the town and its neighbouring areas. Orbus offers regular routes connecting key destinations such as the town centre, Frankton, Arrowtown, and Queenstown Airport. The buses are modern, comfortable, and equipped with features like air conditioning and free Wi-Fi. Travelers can purchase single-ride tickets or multi-trip passes for added convenience.

2. Connectabus

Connectabus is another popular bus service in Queenstown, offering transportation to various destinations within the region. Connectabus operates scheduled services between Queenstown, Arrowtown, Frankton, and other nearby towns and attractions. The buses are wheelchair accessible and provide a reliable way to explore the area's scenic beauty and attractions. Travelers can purchase tickets onboard or through the Connectabus website and app.

3. Water Taxis

For a unique and scenic way to travel around Lake Wakatipu, water taxis offer an unforgettable experience. These taxis operate between Queenstown and destinations such as Walter

Peak Station, providing a picturesque journey across the lake. Passengers can enjoy stunning views of the surrounding mountains and landscapes while travelling in comfort and style.

Car Rentals

1. Rental Agencies

Renting a car is a popular option for travellers who want to explore Queenstown and its surrounding areas at their own pace. Several car rental agencies operate in Queenstown, offering a wide range of vehicles to suit different preferences and budgets. Whether you prefer a compact car for city driving or a four-wheel-drive vehicle for exploring off-road trails, you'll find plenty of options to choose from.

2. Self-Drive Tours

For travellers who enjoy the freedom of independent travel but prefer not to navigate on their own, self-drive tours are an excellent option. Several tour operators in Queenstown offer self-drive tour packages that include a rental car, accommodation, and an itinerary tailored to your interests and preferences. These tours allow you to explore Queenstown and its surrounding areas at your own pace while providing the convenience of pre-planned routes and accommodations.

Cycling and Walking

1. Queenstown Trail

The Queenstown Trail is a network of walking and cycling trails that showcases the region's stunning scenery and attractions. The trail covers over 130 kilometres of terrain, including lakeside paths, riverside trails, and mountain tracks. Whether you're a leisurely walker or an avid cyclist, the Queenstown Trail offers something for everyone. Along the way, you'll encounter historic sites, vineyards, and panoramic viewpoints, providing a unique and immersive way to experience Queenstown's beauty.

2. Bike Rentals

For travellers who want to explore Queenstown on two wheels, bike rentals are readily available in the town centre. Several bike rental shops offer a range of bikes, including mountain bikes, electric bikes, and cruiser bikes, suitable for different terrains and preferences. Many accommodations also provide bike rental services, allowing guests to explore the area at their leisure.

Taxi and Ride-Sharing Services

1. Taxis

Taxis are a convenient option for getting around Queenstown, especially for short trips or late-night travel. Several taxi companies operate in the area, providing prompt and reliable service to travellers. Taxis can be hailed on the street, booked by phone, or arranged through your accommodation. They offer a convenient way to reach destinations that may not be easily accessible by public transport.

2. Ride-Sharing Services

Ride-sharing services like Uber and Lyft are also available in Queenstown, providing an alternative to traditional taxis. These services offer the convenience of booking a ride through a smartphone app, allowing travellers to quickly and easily arrange transportation to their desired destination. Ride-sharing services are particularly popular among visitors who prefer the flexibility and convenience of on-demand transportation.

Getting around Queenstown is easy and convenient, thanks to its efficient transportation options. Whether you prefer public transport, renting a car, cycling and walking, or using taxi and ride-sharing services, Queenstown offers something for every traveller's needs and preferences. With its well-connected network of buses, scenic walking and cycling trails, and convenient taxi and ride-sharing options, exploring

Queenstown and its surrounding areas is a breeze. So, whether you're embarking on a solo adventure, travelling with family and friends, or exploring the region's attractions, transportation in Queenstown ensures a smooth and enjoyable journey from start to finish.

Chapter 5. Top Attractions

Queenstown is renowned for its stunning natural beauty and abundance of outdoor adventures. From towering mountain peaks to crystal-clear lakes and adrenaline-pumping activities, there's no shortage of attractions to explore in this vibrant town. Here are some of the top attractions that should be on every visitor's list when exploring Queenstown.

1. Skyline Queenstown

Skyline Queenstown offers visitors a thrilling experience high above the town, with breathtaking views of Lake Wakatipu and the surrounding mountains. Here, you can hop aboard the Skyline Gondola, which takes you on a scenic ride to the top of Bob's Peak. Once at the summit, you'll find a range of activities to enjoy, including:

Luge

The Skyline Luge is a fun and exciting downhill ride on a three-wheeled cart, suitable for all ages. Race down the purpose-built tracks as you control your speed with a simple handbrake, offering a thrilling experience with stunning panoramic views as your backdrop.

Kiwi Haka

Experience the rich Maori culture with a performance of the Kiwi Haka, a traditional Maori cultural show. Be captivated by powerful performances of song, dance, and storytelling, offering insight into the history, customs, and traditions of New Zealand's indigenous people.

Stratosfare Restaurant

Indulge in a delicious meal at the Stratosfare Restaurant, which offers panoramic views of Queenstown and its surrounding landscapes. Enjoy a buffet-style dining experience featuring a range of local and international cuisine, accompanied by fine wines from the Central Otago region.

Mountain Biking and Walking Trails

For outdoor enthusiasts, Skyline Queenstown offers a network of mountain biking and walking trails with varying difficulty levels. Explore the scenic beauty of Bob's Peak on foot or by bike, with trails that wind through native forests and offer stunning views of Lake Wakatipu and the Remarkables mountain range.

2. Queenstown Gardens

Nestled along the shores of Lake Wakatipu, Queenstown Gardens is a picturesque oasis in the heart of the town. This beautifully landscaped park offers a peaceful retreat from the hustle and bustle of Queenstown, with a variety of attractions and activities to enjoy.

Botanical Gardens

Stroll through the park's botanical gardens, which feature a diverse collection of native and exotic plants, flowers, and trees. Marvel at the vibrant colours and fragrant aromas as you explore the winding paths and lush greenery.

Rose Garden

Admire the beauty of the Queenstown Rose Garden, which boasts over 1,500 roses in a stunning array of colours and varieties. Take a stroll among the fragrant blooms, or find a quiet spot to relax and soak in the tranquil atmosphere.

Disc Golf

For a fun and family-friendly activity, try your hand at disc golf in Queenstown Gardens. The park features a nine-hole disc golf course set amidst the scenic surroundings, offering a challenging and entertaining game for players of all skill levels.

Lakefront Views

Take in the breathtaking views of Lake Wakatipu and the surrounding mountains from Queenstown Gardens. Find a peaceful spot along the lakefront to sit and relax, enjoy a picnic with friends and family, or simply soak in the beauty of nature.

3. The Remarkables

As one of New Zealand's most iconic mountain ranges, The Remarkables offer a stunning backdrop for outdoor adventures in Queenstown. Whether you're a thrill-seeker or a nature lover, there's something for everyone to enjoy amidst these majestic peaks.

Skiing and Snowboarding

During the winter months, The Remarkables transforms into a world-class ski resort, offering some of the best skiing and snowboarding terrain in the Southern Hemisphere. With wide-open slopes, varied terrain, and stunning alpine scenery, it's no wonder that The Remarkables is a favourite destination for winter sports enthusiasts.

Hiking and Scenic Walks

In the summer, The Remarkables are a paradise for hikers and outdoor enthusiasts. Explore a network of hiking trails that wind through alpine meadows, rugged terrain, and stunning vistas. From short scenic walks to challenging alpine hikes, there's a trail for every skill level and interest.

Photography

With its dramatic peaks, sparkling lakes, and ever-changing light, The Remarkables offers endless opportunities for photographers to capture stunning landscapes and breathtaking vistas. Whether you're a professional photographer or simply enjoy taking photos as a hobby, The Remarkables provides a picturesque backdrop for your creative endeavours.

Chairlift Rides

For a unique perspective of The Remarkables, take a scenic chairlift ride to the summit. Sit back and relax as you ascend to breathtaking heights, enjoying panoramic views of Queenstown, Lake Wakatipu, and the surrounding mountains. It's a memorable experience that offers a bird's-eye view of this spectacular alpine landscape.

4. Shotover River

Known for its crystal-clear waters, rugged canyon walls, and thrilling rapids, the Shotover River is a playground for adrenaline junkies and nature enthusiasts alike. Here are some of the top attractions and activities to experience along the Shotover River.

Jet Boating

Experience the ultimate adrenaline rush with a jet boat ride along the Shotover River. Hold on tight as your skilled driver navigates the narrow canyons, twists, and turns, reaching speeds of up to 85 kilometres per hour. Feel the thrill of 360-degree spins and heart-pounding manoeuvres as you explore this scenic river.

White-Water Rafting

For a more immersive adventure, try white-water rafting on the Shotover River. Join a guided tour and paddle through exhilarating rapids, splash through foaming waves, and navigate through narrow canyons. With rapids ranging from grade 3 to 5, the Shotover River offers an exciting challenge for rafters of all levels.

Canyon Swing and Canyon Fox

For the ultimate adrenaline rush, take the plunge with a canyon swing or canyon fox experience over the Shotover

River. Leap from towering cliff edges, freefalling into the abyss before swinging out over the canyon floor. With multiple jump styles and heights to choose from, it's an exhilarating experience that's sure to get your heart racing.

Scenic Walks and Picnic Spots

For those seeking a more leisurely experience, the Shotover River offers several scenic walks and picnic spots along its banks. Take a peaceful stroll along the river's edge, marvelling at the rugged canyon scenery and tranquil waters. Find a quiet spot to enjoy a picnic lunch with friends and family, surrounded by nature's beauty.

Chapter 6. Outdoor Activities

Queenstown, nestled amidst the stunning landscapes of New Zealand's South Island, is a playground for outdoor enthusiasts. From adrenaline-pumping adventures to serene nature walks, there's no shortage of activities to enjoy in this picturesque region. Here are some of the top outdoor activities that Queenstown has to offer.

1. Skiing and Snowboarding

Coronet Peak

Coronet Peak is one of New Zealand's premier ski resorts, offering world-class skiing and snowboarding experiences. With its wide-open slopes, varied terrain, and state-of-the-art facilities, it's no wonder that Coronet Peak is a favourite destination for winter sports enthusiasts. Whether you're a seasoned pro or a first-time skier, there's something for everyone to enjoy at this iconic alpine resort.

The Remarkables

Named for their remarkable beauty, The Remarkables offer some of the best skiing and snowboarding terrain in the Southern Hemisphere. With four distinct ski areas catering to skiers and snowboarders of all levels, The Remarkables provides endless opportunities for adventure and excitement. From gentle beginner slopes to challenging black diamond runs, there's a trail for every skill level and preference.

Cardrona Alpine Resort

Located just a short drive from Queenstown, Cardrona Alpine Resort is a premier destination for skiing and snowboarding. With its wide-open terrain, reliable snowfall, and family-friendly atmosphere, Cardrona offers a welcoming environment for skiers and snowboarders of all ages and abilities. Whether you're hitting the slopes for the first time or honing your skills on challenging runs, Cardrona promises an unforgettable winter sports experience.

2. Hiking and Trekking

Ben Lomond Track

The Ben Lomond Track is one of Queenstown's most popular hiking trails, offering stunning panoramic views of Lake Wakatipu and the surrounding mountains. This challenging hike begins at the Skyline Gondola base station and ascends to the summit of Ben Lomond, reaching an elevation of 1,748 meters. Along the way, hikers will encounter diverse landscapes, including native beech forests, alpine meadows, and rocky ridgelines, providing a rewarding and memorable hiking experience.

Routeburn Track

Considered one of New Zealand's Great Walks, the Routeburn Track is a multi-day hiking trail that traverses the spectacular landscapes of Fiordland National Park. Starting near Glenorchy, just a short drive from Queenstown, the trail winds through pristine beech forests, past cascading waterfalls, and across alpine passes, offering breathtaking views at every turn. Whether you're completing the entire track or embarking on a day hike, the Routeburn Track promises an unforgettable adventure amidst some of New Zealand's most awe-inspiring scenery.

Queenstown Hill

For a shorter hike with equally stunning views, head to Queenstown Hill. This popular hiking trail begins near the town centre and ascends to the summit of Te Tapu-nui (also known as Queenstown Hill), offering panoramic vistas of Lake Wakatipu, the Remarkables, and the surrounding mountains. Along the way, hikers will pass through native beech forests and past historic landmarks, including the famous Basket of Dreams sculpture, making it a scenic and rewarding hike for visitors of all fitness levels.

3. Bungee Jumping

Kawarau Bridge Bungy

As the birthplace of bungee jumping, Queenstown offers adrenaline junkies the chance to take the plunge from the historic Kawarau Bridge. Suspended over the turquoise waters of the Kawarau River, this iconic bungee jump offers a thrilling freefall experience amidst stunning alpine scenery. Whether you're a first-time jumper or a seasoned thrill-seeker, the Kawarau Bridge Bungy promises an exhilarating adventure that will leave you feeling exhilarated and alive.

Nevis Bungy

For the ultimate bungee jumping experience, brave the Nevis Bungy, one of the highest bungee jumps in the world. Located in the remote Nevis Valley, just a short drive from Queenstown, this jaw-dropping jump sees participants leap from a towering platform suspended 134 meters above the rugged canyon floor below. With its breathtaking views and heart-pounding freefall, the Nevis Bungy offers an adrenaline rush like no other, making it a must-do activity for thrill-seekers visiting Queenstown.

4. Jet Boating

Shotover Jet

Experience the thrill of high-speed jet boating on the Shotover River with Shotover Jet, Queenstown's original jet boat ride. Hold on tight as your skilled driver navigates the narrow canyons, twists, and turns, reaching speeds of up to 85 kilometres per hour. Feel the rush of adrenaline as you race past sheer rock walls and towering cliffs, with 360-degree spins and heart-pounding manoeuvres adding to the excitement. With its combination of speed, scenery, and thrills, Shotover Jet offers an unforgettable adventure for visitors of all ages.

5. Paragliding

Coronet Peak Tandems

Soar high above Queenstown with Coronet Peak Tandems, offering tandem paragliding flights amidst the stunning landscapes of the Southern Alps. Take to the skies with an experienced pilot and enjoy panoramic views of Lake Wakatipu, the Remarkables, and the surrounding mountains as you glide gracefully through the air. With its gentle takeoffs and smooth landings, tandem paragliding is suitable for adventurers of all ages and abilities, offering a unique perspective of Queenstown's natural beauty that's sure to take your breath away.

Chapter 7. Adventure Sports

Queenstown is renowned as the adventure capital of New Zealand, offering a plethora of adrenaline-pumping activities for thrill-seekers and outdoor enthusiasts. From heart-stopping skydives to exhilarating white-water rafting, there's no shortage of adventure sports to get your blood pumping in this picturesque region. Here are some of the top adventure sports that Queenstown has to offer.

1. Skydiving

Nzone Skydive Queenstown

Experience the ultimate thrill of skydiving with Nzone Skydive Queenstown, one of New Zealand's premier skydiving operators. Strap on your parachute and take to the skies aboard a purpose-built aircraft, reaching altitudes of up to 15,000 feet. Feel the rush of adrenaline as you freefall at speeds of over 200 kilometres per hour, with panoramic views of Lake Wakatipu, the Remarkables, and the Southern Alps stretching out below. Whether you're a first-time jumper or a seasoned skydiver, Nzone Skydive Queenstown promises an unforgettable experience that will leave you feeling exhilarated and alive.

2. White-Water Rafting

Queenstown Rafting

Embark on a white-water rafting adventure with Queenstown Rafting, exploring the thrilling rapids of the Shotover River. Choose from a range of rafting experiences, from scenic floats to adrenaline-pumping white-water trips, suitable for beginners and experienced rafters alike. Navigate through narrow canyons, splash through foaming waves, and tackle exciting rapids, with experienced guides leading the way and ensuring a safe and enjoyable journey. With its combination of excitement, stunning scenery, and camaraderie, white-water rafting with Queenstown Rafting promises an unforgettable adventure for all.

3. Mountain Biking

Queenstown Bike Park

For mountain biking enthusiasts, Queenstown Bike Park offers an exhilarating network of trails and terrain parks catering to riders of all skill levels. Located at the base of Coronet Peak, just a short drive from Queenstown, the bike park features a variety of downhill tracks, jump lines, and technical trails, providing endless opportunities for adrenaline-fueled fun. Whether you're a beginner honing your skills or an experienced rider seeking thrills, Queenstown Bike Park offers something for everyone, with stunning alpine scenery and panoramic views adding to the excitement.

Arrowtown Trails

Explore the scenic beauty of Arrowtown with its network of mountain biking trails winding through historic gold mining sites, native forests, and picturesque landscapes. From gentle riverside paths to challenging singletrack descents, Arrowtown offers a diverse range of trails suitable for riders of all abilities. Take in the stunning views of the surrounding mountains and valleys as you pedal along winding trails, with opportunities to explore historic landmarks and enjoy a leisurely ride amidst nature's beauty.

4. Ziplining

Ziptrek Ecotours

Soar through the treetops with Ziptrek Ecotours, offering an exhilarating ziplining experience in the heart of Queenstown. Strap on your harness and glide along a series of zip lines suspended high above the forest floor, with panoramic views of the surrounding mountains and Lake Wakatipu below. Feel the rush of adrenaline as you zip from tree to tree, navigating through the forest canopy and experiencing the thrill of flight. With its emphasis on sustainability and eco-friendly practices, Ziptrek Ecotours offers a unique and unforgettable adventure that's as exhilarating as it is environmentally conscious.

Skyline Zipline

For a ziplining adventure with stunning panoramic views, head to Skyline Queenstown and embark on a zipline tour with Skyline Zipline. Soar high above the Queenstown skyline as you zip along a series of cables, enjoying breathtaking views of Lake Wakatipu, the Remarkables, and the surrounding mountains. With multiple zip lines of varying lengths and speeds, as well as suspension bridges and platforms, Skyline Zipline offers an exciting and scenic adventure for thrill-seekers of all ages.

Queenstown's adventure sports scene offers a thrilling array of activities to suit every taste and adrenaline level. Whether you're a skydiving enthusiast, a white-water rafting aficionado, a mountain biking fanatic, or a ziplining daredevil, Queenstown has something for everyone. So, pack your sense of adventure and get ready to experience the adrenaline-fueled excitement of Queenstown's outdoor playground.

Chapter 8. Cultural Experiences in Queenstown

Beyond its reputation as an adventure playground, Queenstown also offers a rich tapestry of cultural experiences that provide insight into New Zealand's history, arts, and traditions. From immersing yourself in Maori culture and history to exploring local art galleries and enjoying live music performances, there's plenty to discover in Queenstown for those seeking a deeper connection with the region's cultural heritage. Let's delve into some of the top cultural experiences awaiting visitors in Queenstown.

1. Maori Culture and History

Te Ao Maori

Discover the rich heritage and traditions of New Zealand's indigenous people, the Maori, through immersive cultural experiences offered in Queenstown. Te Ao Maori provides visitors with an opportunity to learn about Maori history, customs, and practices through interactive workshops, performances, and guided tours. Engage in traditional Maori arts and crafts, learn the haka (war dance), and gain insights into the spiritual significance of Maori symbols and rituals. Te Ao Maori offers a unique opportunity to connect with New Zealand's indigenous culture and gain a deeper appreciation for the land and its people.

Maori Rock Art

Explore the ancient rock art sites scattered throughout the Queenstown region, offering glimpses into the artistic and spiritual practices of the Maori people. These intricate carvings and paintings, created by Maori ancestors hundreds of years ago, depict scenes from daily life, mythology, and spiritual beliefs. Join a guided tour to visit these sacred sites, learn about their cultural significance, and gain a greater understanding of Maori culture and history.

2. Local Art and Music

Central Art Gallery

Immerse yourself in Queenstown's vibrant arts scene at the Central Art Gallery, showcasing works by talented local and national artists. Browse through a diverse collection of paintings, sculptures, ceramics, and mixed-media artworks, with styles ranging from contemporary to traditional. The gallery provides a platform for emerging artists to showcase their talents and offers visitors the opportunity to purchase unique pieces of art to take home as souvenirs. Additionally, the gallery hosts regular exhibitions, artist talks, and workshops, providing opportunities for cultural enrichment and creative exploration.

Live Music Venues

Experience the vibrant sounds of Queenstown's local music scene at various live music venues scattered throughout the town. From cosy pubs and intimate cafes to lively bars and outdoor amphitheatres, there's no shortage of places to enjoy live music performances showcasing a diverse range of genres, from folk and jazz to rock and electronic. Whether you're looking to unwind with acoustic melodies, dance the night away to upbeat rhythms, or discover emerging local talent, Queenstown's live music venues offer something for every music lover.

3. Museums and Galleries

Lakes District Museum

Step back in time and explore Queenstown's fascinating history at the Lakes District Museum, housed in a historic stone building dating back to the gold rush era. The museum features a diverse collection of artefacts, photographs, and interactive exhibits that trace the region's heritage from its Maori roots to its colonial past and beyond. Learn about the impact of the gold rush on Queenstown's development, discover stories of pioneering settlers and indigenous inhabitants, and gain insights into the cultural, social, and economic forces that have shaped the town's identity.

Milford Galleries

Discover contemporary New Zealand art at Milford Galleries, a leading contemporary art gallery showcasing works by established and emerging artists from across the country. Located in the heart of Queenstown, the gallery features a dynamic selection of paintings, sculptures, ceramics, and multimedia installations that reflect the diversity and creativity of New Zealand's artistic landscape. Whether you're a seasoned art enthusiast or a casual observer, Milford Galleries offers a stimulating and thought-provoking experience that celebrates the power of visual expression.

Queenstown's cultural experiences offer a captivating glimpse into the region's rich heritage and artistic diversity. Whether you're exploring Maori culture and history, immersing yourself in local art and music, or delving into the town's museum and gallery scene, there's something to inspire and delight visitors of all interests and backgrounds. So, take the time to immerse yourself in Queenstown's cultural offerings and discover the stories, traditions, and artistic expressions that make this vibrant town truly unique.

Chapter 9. Exploring Queenstown's Food and Drink Scene

Queenstown isn't just a haven for adventure seekers; it's also a culinary hotspot that tantalizes taste buds with its diverse array of flavours and dining experiences. From must-try local dishes to top-notch restaurants, wineries, and farmers markets, Queenstown offers a gastronomic journey that's as exciting as it is delicious. Let's dive into the vibrant food and drink scene of Queenstown.

Must-Try Local Dishes

Fergburger

No visit to Queenstown is complete without sinking your teeth into a Fergburger, the town's iconic gourmet burger joint. Sink your teeth into the succulent patties sandwiched between fluffy buns, with creative toppings like blue cheese, aioli, and pineapple relish. Be prepared to queue, but trust us, the wait is worth it for a taste of Queenstown's most famous burger.

Venison

Queenstown's lush landscapes are home to abundant wildlife, including deer, making venison a local speciality. Head to one of the town's top restaurants to savour tender venison steaks or slow-cooked venison stews, paired with locally sourced ingredients and complemented by New Zealand wines.

Fruits of the Sea

With its proximity to pristine waters, Queenstown boasts a bounty of fresh seafood, from succulent green-lipped mussels to plump crayfish and sweet Bluff oysters. Indulge in a seafood feast at one of the town's seafood restaurants, where you can savour the flavours of the ocean while enjoying panoramic views of Lake Wakatipu.

Top Restaurants and Cafes

Rata

Owned by renowned New Zealand chef Josh Emett, Rata offers contemporary New Zealand cuisine in an elegant yet relaxed setting. Dine on innovative dishes crafted from locally sourced ingredients, such as Otago lamb, Fiordland venison, and South Island salmon, paired with an extensive selection of New Zealand wines.

Amisfield Bistro & Cellar Door

Set amidst picturesque vineyards in nearby Lake Hayes, Amisfield Bistro & Cellar Door offers a farm-to-table dining experience with stunning views of the surrounding mountains.

Feast on seasonal dishes inspired by the region's bounty, accompanied by award-winning wines from the Amisfield vineyard.

Vudu Cafe & Larder

For a casual breakfast or lunch spot, head to Vudu Cafe & Larder, a beloved local institution known for its delicious coffee, freshly baked pastries, and hearty brunch fare. Situated in the heart of Queenstown, Vudu is the perfect place to fuel up before a day of adventure or relax with friends over a leisurely meal.

Wineries and Craft Breweries

Gibbston Valley Winery

Venture into the scenic Gibbston Valley, known as the "Valley of the Vines," to discover Gibbston Valley Winery, one of Central Otago's premier wine producers. Take a guided tour of the winery's vineyards and cellar, followed by a tasting of their award-winning Pinot Noirs, Rieslings, and Chardonnays, paired with gourmet cheese platters and local delicacies.

Altitude Brewing

Sample handcrafted brews with a view at Altitude Brewing, Queenstown's craft brewery located in the heart of the town. From hoppy IPAs to refreshing lagers and rich stouts, Altitude

Brewing offers a diverse range of beers to suit every palate. Pull up a stool at the brewery's tasting room and enjoy a flight of their latest brews while taking in panoramic views of the Remarkables mountain range.

Farmers Markets

Remarkables Market

Experience the vibrant flavours and colours of Queenstown's local produce at the Remarkables Market, held every Saturday in the Remarkables Park Town Centre. Browse stalls brimming with fresh fruits and vegetables, artisanal cheeses, organic meats, homemade preserves, and baked goods, sourced directly from local farmers, producers, and artisans. Enjoy live music, cooking demonstrations, and family-friendly activities while soaking up the lively atmosphere of this bustling market.

Queenstown Farmers Market

Discover the best of Queenstown's seasonal produce at the Queenstown Farmers Market, held every Saturday in the Queenstown Gardens. Browse stalls overflowing with farm-fresh fruits and vegetables, free-range eggs, locally caught seafood, artisanal bread, and gourmet treats. Sample homemade jams, chutneys, and sauces, and chat with friendly vendors who are passionate about their products and eager to share their knowledge with visitors.

Queenstown's food and drink scene is a feast for the senses, offering a tantalizing array of flavours, cuisines, and experiences to suit every taste and budget. Whether you're indulging in local delicacies, dining at top-notch restaurants, sampling wines at scenic vineyards, or browsing the stalls at bustling farmers' markets, Queenstown promises a culinary adventure that's sure to leave you craving more. So, come hungry and prepare to be delighted by the flavours of Queenstown!

Chapter 10. Shopping in Queenstown: A Retail Adventure

Queenstown isn't just a destination for outdoor adventure and culinary delights; it's also a shopper's paradise, offering a diverse array of retail experiences that cater to every taste and style. Whether you're in search of unique souvenirs, fashionable apparel, or locally crafted treasures, Queenstown's shopping scene has something to delight every shopper. Let's embark on a retail adventure through the charming streets and bustling markets of Queenstown.

Souvenir Shops

Creative Queenstown Arts and Crafts Market

Immerse yourself in Queenstown's vibrant arts and crafts scene at the Creative Queenstown Arts and Crafts Market, held every Saturday in Earnslaw Park. Browse stalls brimming with handmade jewellery, pottery, textiles, woodwork, and other artisanal creations crafted by local artists and craftspeople. From intricate Maori carvings to colourful woven textiles and quirky ceramics, you'll find a treasure trove of unique souvenirs to commemorate your visit to Queenstown.

Remarkables Market
Discover the best of Queenstown's local produce and artisanal goods at the Remarkables Market, held every Saturday in the Remarkables Park Town Centre. Browse stalls offering a diverse range of products, including handmade soaps and skin care products, gourmet food and wine, handcrafted candles and homewares, and much more. Whether you're looking for a tasty treat, a unique gift, or a keepsake to remind you of your time in Queenstown, the Remarkables Market has something for everyone.

Fashion and Apparel

Queenstown Mall

Explore the bustling streets of Queenstown Mall, lined with an eclectic mix of boutique stores, fashion retailers, and designer boutiques. From high-end fashion labels to locally owned boutiques showcasing the latest trends, Queenstown Mall offers a diverse range of shopping options for fashion enthusiasts. Whether you're in search of stylish streetwear, outdoor adventure gear, or elegant evening wear, you'll find plenty to tempt you as you stroll through the town centre.

Outside Sports

Gear up for outdoor adventure at Outside Sports, Queenstown's premier destination for outdoor apparel and equipment. From hiking boots and ski gear to waterproof jackets and technical clothing, Outside Sports offers everything you need to embrace the great outdoors in style and comfort. Browse top outdoor brands like The North Face, Patagonia, and Icebreaker, and receive expert advice from knowledgeable staff who are passionate about outdoor pursuits.

Local Artisans and Crafts

Queenstown Arts Centre

Discover the creative talents of Queenstown's local artisans at the Queenstown Arts Centre, located in the historic Old Dairy Building. Explore a diverse range of arts and crafts, including paintings, sculptures, ceramics, jewellery, textiles, and more, all handmade by local artists and craftspeople. Attend art exhibitions, workshops, and events hosted by the arts centre, and immerse yourself in Queenstown's thriving arts community.

Ivy & Arrow

Step inside Ivy & Arrow, a charming boutique showcasing a curated selection of handmade goods crafted by local artisans and designers. From hand-poured candles and natural skincare products to handcrafted jewellery and leather goods, Ivy & Arrow offers a range of unique and thoughtfully crafted treasures that celebrate the beauty and creativity of Queenstown's artisan community. Whether you're shopping for yourself or searching for the perfect gift, you'll find plenty of inspiration at Ivy & Arrow.

Queenstown's shopping scene offers a delightful mix of local charm, artisanal craftsmanship, and international flair, making it a must-visit destination for shoppers of all interests and tastes. Whether you're browsing the stalls at bustling markets, exploring boutique stores in the town centre, or discovering handmade treasures at local artisans' workshops, Queenstown promises a retail experience that's as unique and memorable as the town itself. So, lace up your walking shoes, grab your shopping bags, and prepare to embark on a retail adventure through the picturesque streets and vibrant markets of Queenstown.

Chapter 11. Day Trips and Excursions: Exploring Queenstown's Surroundings

While Queenstown offers plenty of excitement within its borders, venturing beyond the town limits unveils a world of natural wonders, historic charm, and breathtaking landscapes waiting to be explored. From the majestic beauty of Milford Sound to the quaint streets of Arrowtown and the serene shores of Lake Wanaka, there's no shortage of day trips and excursions to embark on from Queenstown. Let's embark on a journey through some of the most captivating destinations surrounding Queenstown.

Milford Sound

Awe-Inspiring Beauty

Embark on a scenic journey through Fiordland National Park to reach Milford Sound, one of New Zealand's most iconic natural attractions. Cruise along the tranquil waters of the fiord, framed by towering cliffs, cascading waterfalls, and lush rainforest. Marvel at the beauty of Mitre Peak, the tallest peak in the region, and keep an eye out for wildlife such as seals, dolphins, and penguins. Milford Sound is a UNESCO World Heritage Site and a testament to the raw, untamed beauty of New Zealand's wilderness.

Activities

In addition to cruising, Milford Sound offers a variety of activities to immerse yourself in the stunning surroundings. Embark on a guided kayak tour to explore the fiord up close, paddle beneath towering waterfalls, and discover hidden coves and inlets. Alternatively, take to the skies on a scenic flight over Milford Sound, offering bird's-eye views of its dramatic landscapes, including the iconic Mitre Peak and the stunning Sutherland Falls.

Arrowtown

Historic Charm

Step back in time as you explore the charming streets of Arrowtown, a historic gold mining town located just a short drive from Queenstown. Wander along tree-lined avenues lined with quaint cottages, browse boutique shops housed in historic buildings, and soak up the town's rich heritage at the Arrowtown Museum. Learn about the area's gold rush history, visit historic sites such as the Chinese Settlement, and stroll through tranquil parks and gardens dotted with autumnal colours.

Local Cuisine

Indulge in delicious local cuisine at Arrowtown's cafes and restaurants, offering a variety of dining options to suit every palate. Sample hearty comfort food at a traditional pub, savour artisanal dishes made from locally sourced ingredients or treat yourself to homemade baked goods and sweet treats at a cosy cafe. Don't miss the opportunity to try Arrowtown's famous pies, a beloved local delicacy that's perfect for a quick and tasty snack on the go.

Glenorchy

Spectacular Scenery

Journey to the picturesque village of Glenorchy, nestled at the northern end of Lake Wakatipu and surrounded by snow-capped mountains and pristine wilderness. Known for its breathtaking scenery, Glenorchy has served as the backdrop for numerous films, including "The Lord of the Rings" and

"The Hobbit" trilogies, thanks to its dramatic landscapes and untouched beauty. Take a scenic drive along the Glenorchy-Queenstown Road, stopping at viewpoints to capture photos of the stunning scenery.

Outdoor Adventures

Glenorchy is a haven for outdoor enthusiasts, offering a range of activities to suit every taste and skill level. Explore the surrounding wilderness on a guided horse trek, hike along scenic trails in the nearby Mount Aspiring National Park, or embark on a thrilling jet boat ride along the Dart River. For a truly unique experience, take a guided tour to Paradise, a remote area of the region known for its pristine beauty and untouched landscapes, where you can immerse yourself in the tranquillity of nature and discover hidden gems off the beaten path.

Lake Wanaka

Serene Beauty

Escape the hustle and bustle of Queenstown and discover the serene beauty of Lake Wanaka, located just a scenic drive away. Framed by snow-capped peaks and surrounded by native bushland, Lake Wanaka offers a peaceful retreat amidst nature's splendour. Take a stroll along the lakeside walking tracks, picnic on the shores of the lake, or simply relax and soak up the tranquillity of this idyllic setting.

Water Activities

Lake Wanaka is a paradise for water lovers, offering a variety of activities to enjoy on its crystal-clear waters. Rent a kayak, paddleboard, or boat and explore the lake at your own pace, discovering hidden bays, secluded beaches, and rocky coves along the way. Alternatively, try your hand at fishing and reel in trout or salmon from the depths of the lake, or embark on a scenic cruise to enjoy panoramic views of the surrounding mountains and landscapes.

Each of these day trips and excursions offers a unique opportunity to explore the diverse landscapes, rich heritage, and natural beauty surrounding Queenstown. Whether you're cruising through the majestic fiords of Milford Sound, wandering the historic streets of Arrowtown, soaking up the tranquillity of Glenorchy, or admiring the serene beauty of Lake Wanaka, you're sure to create unforgettable memories that will last a lifetime. So, pack your sense of adventure and embark on a journey of discovery through the stunning surroundings of Queenstown.

Chapter 12. Embracing the Seasons: Queenstown's Seasonal Highlights

Queenstown's beauty knows no bounds, and each season brings its own set of delights, from vibrant festivals and outdoor adventures to stunning natural displays. Whether you're basking in the summer sunshine, carving up the slopes in winter, or admiring the colours of autumn and the blooms of spring, Queenstown offers something special to experience in every season. Let's explore the seasonal highlights that make Queenstown a year-round destination.

Summer Festivals and Events

Summer Concert Series

As the temperatures rise and the days grow longer, Queenstown comes alive with a host of summer festivals and events. One of the highlights is the Summer Concert Series, featuring live music performances by local and international artists against the backdrop of Queenstown's stunning scenery. From open-air concerts in the park to intimate gigs at waterfront venues, the Summer Concert Series offers a diverse lineup of musical genres to suit every taste.

Queenstown Winter Festival

Celebrate the arrival of summer with the Queenstown Winter Festival, a lively celebration of community, culture, and creativity. Spanning ten days, the festival features a packed schedule of events, including street parades, live music performances, outdoor concerts, food and wine tastings, and family-friendly activities. Join locals and visitors alike as they come together to celebrate the spirit of Queenstown and kick off the summer season in style.

Adventure Activities

With long sunny days and mild temperatures, summer is the perfect time to indulge in outdoor adventures in Queenstown. From hiking and mountain biking to water sports and scenic flights, there's no shortage of activities to enjoy amidst the stunning landscapes of the region. Take a scenic cruise on Lake Wakatipu, paddleboard along the tranquil waters, or soar high above the mountains on a tandem paragliding flight. With its endless array of adventures, Queenstown promises an unforgettable summer experience for thrill-seekers and nature lovers alike.

Winter Sports Season

Skiing and Snowboarding

Winter is synonymous with skiing and snowboarding in Queenstown, as the region transforms into a winter wonderland with its snow-capped peaks and world-class ski resorts. Hit the slopes at Coronet Peak, The Remarkables, or Cardrona Alpine Resort, where you'll find a variety of terrain suitable for skiers and snowboarders of all levels. Whether you're carving up groomed trails, tackling challenging runs, or practising your tricks in the terrain park, Queenstown's ski fields offer endless opportunities for winter fun and adventure.

Queenstown Winter Festival

Embrace the magic of winter at the Queenstown Winter Festival, a highlight of the winter sports season that celebrates all things snow and ice. Join in the festivities with street parties, fireworks displays, snow sculpting competitions, and après-ski events, as Queenstown comes alive with the energy and excitement of the season. Warm up with mulled wine, hearty soups, and cosy fireside gatherings, and immerse yourself in the festive atmosphere of this iconic winter celebration.

Snowshoeing and Snowmobiling

For a unique winter adventure, venture off the beaten path and explore Queenstown's snow-covered landscapes on snowshoes or snowmobiles. Strap on a pair of snowshoes and trek through pristine snowfields, immersing yourself in the tranquillity of the winter wilderness and enjoying panoramic views of the surrounding mountains. Alternatively, hop on a snowmobile and zoom across open fields, carving through powder and experiencing the thrill of high-speed winter travel. With its combination of adventure and adrenaline, snowshoeing and snowmobiling offer an exciting way to explore Queenstown's winter wonderland.

Spring and Autumn Activities

Foliage Viewing

Spring and autumn bring a kaleidoscope of colours to Queenstown's landscapes, as the foliage bursts into vibrant hues of green, gold, and red. Take a leisurely drive through the countryside to admire the changing colours of the trees, or embark on a hike along scenic trails that wind through native forests and alpine meadows. Don't forget to bring your camera to capture the beauty of Queenstown's autumnal and springtime landscapes, as the region transitions between seasons in a stunning display of natural beauty.

Wine Tasting Tours

Spring and autumn are also ideal times to explore Queenstown's renowned wine regions, where vineyards come to life with the promise of new growth and harvest. Join a wine-tasting tour and visit local wineries and cellar doors, where you can sample award-winning wines, meet the winemakers, and learn about the art of winemaking. Savour the flavours of Central Otago's world-class Pinot Noirs, Rieslings, and Chardonnays, and enjoy panoramic views of the vineyards and surrounding mountains as you sip and swirl your way through Queenstown's wine country.

Cycling Adventures

With mild temperatures and clear skies, spring and autumn are perfect seasons for cycling adventures in Queenstown. Explore the region's scenic trails and picturesque landscapes on two wheels, pedalling along lakeside paths, riverside tracks, and mountain biking trails that offer breathtaking views at every turn. Whether you're a leisurely cyclist or a seasoned rider, Queenstown offers a variety of cycling experiences to suit every skill level and preference, from gentle family-friendly rides to adrenaline-pumping downhill descents.

Queenstown's seasonal highlights offer something special to experience every season, from vibrant festivals and outdoor adventures to stunning natural displays and cultural celebrations. Whether you're soaking up the summer sunshine, carving up the slopes in winter, or admiring the colours of autumn and the blooms of spring, Queenstown promises unforgettable experiences that will leave you not to forget your experience. So, embrace the seasons and embark on a journey of discovery through the breathtaking landscapes and vibrant culture of Queen

Chapter 13. Family-Friendly Adventures in Queenstown

Queenstown isn't just for adrenaline junkies and outdoor enthusiasts; it's also a fantastic destination for families looking to create unforgettable memories together. With a wide range of kid-friendly attractions, parks, and educational experiences, Queenstown offers plenty of opportunities for families to bond, explore, and have fun together. Let's dive into some of the top family-friendly activities that Queenstown has to offer.

Kid-Friendly Attractions

Kiwi Birdlife Park

Immerse your family in the fascinating world of New Zealand's native wildlife at the Kiwi Birdlife Park. Located in the heart of Queenstown, this wildlife sanctuary is home to a variety of native birds, reptiles, and mammals, including the iconic kiwi bird. Explore natural habitats, interactive exhibits, and daily animal encounters, where you can meet kiwis, tuataras, keas, and more. Don't miss the opportunity to participate in conservation efforts and learn about the importance of protecting New Zealand's unique biodiversity.

Skyline Queenstown

Embark on a scenic gondola ride to Skyline Queenstown, where the whole family can enjoy panoramic views of Lake Wakatipu and the surrounding mountains. Once at the top, kids will love the thrilling downhill ride on the Luge track, where they can race each other down the winding tracks and enjoy the adrenaline rush of high-speed twists and turns. Afterwards, take a stroll along the Skyline Treetop Walk, where suspension bridges and viewing platforms offer stunning views of the forest canopy below.

Parks and Playgrounds

Queenstown Gardens

Spend a day exploring the picturesque Queenstown Gardens, a tranquil oasis nestled on the shores of Lake Wakatipu. Pack a picnic and enjoy a leisurely lunch on the grassy lawns, or take a stroll along the walking tracks that wind through native bushland and colourful flower gardens. Kids will love the playgrounds scattered throughout the park, featuring swings, slides, and climbing frames, as well as the miniature steam train that offers rides around the gardens during the summer months.

Frankton Beach

Head to Frankton Beach for a fun-filled day of sun, sand, and water play. Located just a short drive from Queenstown, this family-friendly beach offers calm waters and sandy shores, perfect for swimming, paddling, and building sandcastles. Let the kids splash in the shallows, explore the rock pools, or try their hand at fishing off the jetty. With barbecue facilities, picnic areas, and a grassy foreshore, Frankton Beach is the ideal spot for a relaxed day by the lake with the whole family.

Educational Experiences

Underwater Observatory

Dive beneath the surface of Lake Wakatipu and discover the underwater world at the Underwater Observatory. Located at the end of the Queenstown Wharf, this unique attraction offers a glimpse into the lake's fascinating aquatic ecosystem, with panoramic underwater views of native fish, eels, and plant life. Kids can learn about the lake's geology, ecology, and conservation efforts through interactive exhibits and guided tours, gaining a deeper appreciation for the natural wonders of Lake Wakatipu.

Lakes District Museum

Step back in time and explore Queenstown's rich history at the Lakes District Museum, where interactive exhibits, artefacts, and multimedia displays bring the region's past to life. Kids can dress up in period costumes, try their hand at gold panning, and explore replica gold mining tunnels, gaining insights into Queenstown's gold rush era and pioneering heritage. With its hands-on activities and educational programs, the Lakes District Museum offers a fun and engaging learning experience for the whole family.

Queenstown's family-friendly activities offer something for everyone, from thrilling adventures and outdoor exploration to educational experiences and cultural immersion. Whether you're bonding over a scenic gondola ride, splashing in the waters of Lake Wakatipu, or learning about New Zealand's native wildlife and rich history, Queenstown promises unforgettable moments and cherished memories for families of all ages. So pack your bags, gather the kids, and embark on a family adventure in the breathtaking landscapes and vibrant culture of Queenstown.

Chapter 14. Embracing Wellness and Relaxation in Queenstown

Amidst the adrenaline-pumping adventures and scenic beauty of Queenstown lies a tranquil oasis dedicated to rejuvenation and relaxation. From luxurious spas and wellness centres to serene yoga studios and rejuvenating hot springs, Queenstown offers an array of options for those seeking to unwind and recharge amidst the stunning landscapes of the region. Let's explore the wellness and relaxation experiences that await in Queenstown.

Spas and Wellness Centers

Onsen Hot Pools

Nestled amidst the scenic surrounds of Arthur's Point, Onsen Hot Pools offers a serene escape from the hustle and bustle of daily life. Relax in private cedar-lined hot pools overlooking the Shotover River canyon, where you can soak in the soothing mineral waters and soak up the panoramic views of the surrounding mountains. Choose from a range of indulgent packages that include massage treatments, facials, and other pampering experiences, and emerge feeling refreshed, rejuvenated, and ready to take on the world.

The Spa at Millbrook Resort

Indulge in a world of luxury and relaxation at The Spa at Millbrook Resort, a tranquil haven nestled within the beautiful grounds of Millbrook Resort. Treat yourself to a bespoke spa experience that combines traditional therapies with modern techniques, from massages and body wraps to facials and beauty treatments. Unwind in the spa's sauna, steam room, and outdoor hot tub, or take a dip in the heated lap pool surrounded by lush gardens. With its serene ambience and attentive service, The Spa at Millbrook Resort offers a truly indulgent escape for body, mind, and soul.

Yoga and Meditation

Yoga Nadi

Find your inner peace and harmony at Yoga Nadi, Queenstown's premier yoga studio located in the heart of the town centre. Offering a variety of classes for all levels, from beginner-friendly hatha yoga to dynamic vinyasa flow, Yoga Nadi provides a supportive and welcoming environment for practitioners of all backgrounds and abilities. Immerse yourself in the practice of yoga and meditation, and leave feeling grounded, balanced, and centred in body and mind.

The Sherwood

Discover holistic wellness at The Sherwood, a sustainable hotel and retreat centre located on the shores of Lake Wakatipu. Join daily yoga and meditation classes led by experienced instructors, and practice mindfulness and relaxation amidst the natural beauty of the surrounding landscape. Afterwards, indulge in a nourishing meal at The Sherwood's organic restaurant, where locally sourced ingredients and seasonal flavours take centre stage. Whether you're seeking to deepen your yoga practice, relax and recharge, or simply connect with nature, The Sherwood offers a transformative retreat experience that nourishes the body, mind, and spirit.

Hot Springs and Pools

Hanmer Springs Thermal Pools & Spa
Escape to the picturesque alpine village of Hanmer Springs, located just a scenic drive from Queenstown, and immerse yourself in the rejuvenating waters of Hanmer Springs Thermal Pools & Spa. Relax in a series of natural thermal pools, ranging from soothing mineral pools to invigorating rock pools and water slides. Treat yourself to a spa treatment or massage at the onsite spa, and indulge in a day of pure relaxation amidst the tranquil surroundings of the Southern Alps.

Tekapo Springs
Embark on a scenic drive to Lake Tekapo and soak in the revitalizing waters of Tekapo Springs, a premier hot springs complex nestled on the shores of Lake Tekapo. Relax in the natural mineral waters of the hot pools, which offer stunning views of the lake and surrounding mountains. Unwind in the steam and sauna rooms, or take a plunge in the freshwater pools and enjoy a leisurely swim. With its serene ambience and breathtaking scenery, Tekapo Springs offers a blissful retreat for those seeking relaxation and rejuvenation.

Queenstown's wellness and relaxation offerings provide a welcome respite from the hustle and bustle of everyday life, inviting visitors to unwind, recharge, and connect with their inner selves amidst the stunning landscapes of the region.

Whether you're soaking in the therapeutic waters of a hot spring, practising yoga and meditation in a serene studio, or indulging in a pampering spa treatment, Queenstown offers a variety of experiences to promote wellness and rejuvenation for body, mind, and soul. So take a moment to prioritize self-care and embrace the healing power of relaxation in the breathtaking surroundings of Queenstown.

Chapter 15. Unveiling the Vibrant Nightlife of Queenstown

When the sun sets behind the majestic peaks of the Southern Alps, Queenstown comes alive with an electric energy that pulses through its streets and venues. From cosy bars and lively pubs to bustling nightclubs and world-class entertainment venues, Queenstown offers a diverse array of nightlife options to suit every taste and mood. Let's delve into the bustling nightlife and entertainment scene that awaits in this vibrant alpine town.

Bars and Pubs

The World Bar

Step into The World Bar and prepare to be transported to a world of eclectic charm and vibrant energy. Located in the heart of Queenstown, this iconic establishment is known for its lively atmosphere, innovative cocktails, and welcoming hospitality. Sip on creative concoctions like the "Kiwi Jam Jar" or the "Smoked Maple Old Fashioned" as you soak up the lively ambience and mingle with locals and travellers alike. With regular live music performances and a lively outdoor courtyard, The World Bar is the perfect spot to kick off a night of revelry in Queenstown.

The Bunker

Tucked away in a historic building on Cow Lane, The Bunker offers a sophisticated yet relaxed setting for an evening of cocktails and conversation. Settle into one of the plush leather sofas or pull up a stool at the elegant bar, where skilled mixologists craft artisanal cocktails using premium spirits and locally sourced ingredients. From classic concoctions like the "Negroni" to signature creations like the "Queenstown Mule," The Bunker promises a memorable drinking experience in an intimate and stylish setting.

Live Music Venues

The Sherwood
Experience the vibrant music scene of Queenstown at The Sherwood, a sustainable hotel and cultural hub located on the shores of Lake Wakatipu. With its cosy fireplace, rustic decor, and stunning lake views, The Sherwood provides the perfect backdrop for intimate live music performances by local and touring artists. From acoustic sets in the cosy lounge to outdoor concerts on the lakeside lawn, The Sherwood offers a diverse lineup of musical genres and styles to suit every taste.

Queenstown Arts Centre
Immerse yourself in the local arts scene at the Queenstown Arts Centre, where live music performances, concerts, and cultural events are held throughout the year. From jazz and blues to folk and indie rock, the Arts Centre showcases a variety of musical talents from Queenstown and beyond. Check the event calendar for upcoming performances and concerts, and experience the magic of live music in the heart of Queenstown's creative community.

Nightclubs

Loco

Get ready to dance the night away at Loco, Queenstown's premier nightclub and party destination. With its state-of-the-art sound system, dazzling light shows, and energetic atmosphere, Loco promises an unforgettable nightlife experience for club-goers and party enthusiasts. Dance to the beats of top DJs and guest performers, sip on craft cocktails at the stylish bar and mingle with a diverse crowd of locals and visitors as you embrace the vibrant nightlife of Queenstown.

Cowboys

Saddle up and head to Cowboys, Queenstown's favourite country-themed nightclub and late-night venue. Decked out in rustic decor and cowboy memorabilia, Cowboys offers a unique and lively atmosphere that's perfect for letting loose and having fun. Dance to country hits and top 40 tunes on the spacious dance floor, challenge your friends to a game of pool or darts or kick back with a cold beer on the outdoor patio. With its friendly vibe and energetic ambience, Cowboys promises a night of wild-west fun and entertainment in the heart of Queenstown.

Casino

SkyCity Queenstown Casino

Experience the thrill of gaming at SkyCity Queenstown Casino, where excitement and entertainment await around every corner. Located in the heart of Queenstown, this premier gaming destination offers a wide range of table games, slot machines, and electronic gaming machines for players of all levels. Test your luck at blackjack, roulette, or poker, or try your hand at the latest slot machines and gaming technology. With its stylish decor, attentive service, and lively atmosphere, SkyCity Queenstown Casino provides an unforgettable gaming experience in the heart of the action.

From vibrant bars and pubs to lively nightclubs and world-class entertainment venues, Queenstown's nightlife scene offers something for everyone, whether you're seeking live music, dancing, or gaming excitement. Soak up the lively atmosphere of local hotspots like The World Bar and The Bunker, dance the night away at energetic nightclubs like Loco and Cowboys, or test your luck at SkyCity Queenstown Casino. Whatever your preference, Queenstown promises a night of excitement, entertainment, and unforgettable memories in this dynamic alpine town.

Chapter 16. Navigating Practical Matters in Queenstown: Your Essential Guide

As you embark on your adventure to Queenstown, it's essential to be equipped with practical information to ensure a smooth and enjoyable experience. From understanding the local currency and banking system to staying informed about health and safety precautions, as well as staying connected with internet and communication options, and knowing emergency contacts, here's everything you need to know to navigate the practical aspects of your journey in Queenstown.

Currency and Banking

Currency

The official currency of New Zealand is the New Zealand Dollar (NZD). Denominations include coins (cents) and banknotes (dollars). While credit cards are widely accepted in Queenstown, it's advisable to carry some cash for smaller transactions, especially in rural areas or at markets.

Banking

Queenstown has several banks and ATMs scattered throughout the town centre, making it convenient to access banking services and withdraw cash. Commonly found banks include ANZ, ASB, BNZ, and Westpac, which offer a range of services including currency exchange, ATM facilities, and international money transfers. Banking hours typically run from Monday to Friday, with some branches open on Saturdays.

Health and Safety

Health Precautions

Queenstown boasts a high standard of healthcare facilities, including medical centres, pharmacies, and hospitals. It's advisable to have travel insurance that covers medical emergencies while visiting New Zealand. Additionally, tap water in Queenstown is safe to drink, so you can refill your water bottle from taps and drinking fountains around town.

Safety Tips

Queenstown is generally a safe destination for travellers, but it's essential to take precautions to ensure your safety. Be mindful of your belongings, especially in crowded areas or tourist hotspots, and avoid leaving valuables unattended. When hiking or participating in outdoor activities, be prepared for changing weather conditions and follow safety guidelines provided by local authorities.

Internet and Communication

Internet Access

Queenstown offers reliable internet access, with many cafes, restaurants, and accommodations providing free Wi-Fi for guests. Additionally, you can purchase prepaid SIM cards from local providers such as Spark, Vodafone, and 2degrees, which offer data plans for mobile internet access.

Communication

New Zealand's country code is +64, and Queenstown's area code is 03. When making local calls, you only need to dial the seven-digit phone number. For international calls, dial the international access code (usually 00), followed by the country code, area code (without the leading 0), and phone number. Public payphones are available throughout Queenstown, accepting coins, prepaid phone cards, and credit cards.

Emergency Contacts

Emergency Services

In case of emergencies, dial 111 for immediate assistance from police, fire, or ambulance services. Queenstown has a police station located in the town centre, and emergency services are available 24/7 to respond to any urgent situations. It's essential to know your location and provide clear details when contacting emergency services for assistance.

Medical Assistance

For non-life-threatening medical issues, you can visit one of Queenstown's medical centres or pharmacies for assistance. If you require urgent medical attention, dial 111 or visit the Lakes District Hospital located in nearby Frankton, which provides emergency medical care and services.

Consular Assistance

For consular assistance and support, travellers can contact their respective embassy or consulate in New Zealand. Consular services may include assistance with lost or stolen passports, medical emergencies, legal issues, and other consular matters.

Armed with practical information about currency and banking, health and safety precautions, internet and communication options, and emergency contacts, you're well-prepared to navigate the ins and outs of your journey in Queenstown. Remember to stay vigilant, take necessary precautions, and enjoy the stunning landscapes, exciting activities, and warm hospitality that Queenstown has to offer. Whether you're exploring the town centre, embarking on outdoor adventures, or simply soaking up the local culture, Queenstown promises an unforgettable experience that will leave you with cherished memories for years to come.

Chapter 17. Embracing Sustainable Travel: Tips for Responsible Exploration in Queenstown

As travellers, it's essential to minimize our impact on the environment and local communities while exploring the world. In Queenstown, surrounded by pristine natural beauty, adopting sustainable travel practices is crucial to preserving the region's ecological integrity and cultural heritage. Here are some tips for practising responsible and sustainable travel during your visit to Queenstown.

Eco-Friendly Accommodation

Choose Green-Certified Hotels and Lodges
Opt for accommodations that prioritize sustainability and eco-friendliness. Look for hotels and lodges that have obtained green certifications, such as EarthCheck or Qualmark Enviro, which adhere to strict environmental standards in areas such as energy efficiency, waste management, and water conservation. Many eco-friendly accommodations in Queenstown offer sustainable amenities, such as energy-efficient lighting, water-saving fixtures, and eco-friendly toiletries.

Stay in Eco-Lodges and Eco-Resorts
Consider staying in eco-lodges or eco-resorts that are designed with sustainability in mind. These establishments often incorporate renewable energy sources, such as solar or wind power, and utilize eco-friendly building materials and practices. Eco-lodges may also offer immersive experiences that connect guests with nature, such as guided nature walks, wildlife viewing tours, and educational programs on conservation and environmental stewardship.

Responsible Wildlife Viewing

Choose Ethical Wildlife Tours and Experiences

When participating in wildlife tours and experiences, prioritize ethical and responsible operators that prioritize animal welfare and conservation. Avoid activities that involve captive or exploited animals, such as elephant rides or dolphin shows, and opt for experiences that focus on observing animals in their natural habitats. Look for operators that adhere to wildlife viewing guidelines and regulations, such as maintaining a safe distance from animals and minimizing disturbances to their habitats.

Support Conservation Initiatives

Support local conservation efforts and organizations that work to protect wildlife and their habitats in Queenstown and the surrounding areas. Consider donating to wildlife conservation projects, volunteering with conservation organizations, or participating in citizen science programs that contribute to ongoing research and monitoring efforts. By supporting conservation initiatives, you can help preserve the region's biodiversity and ensure that future generations can continue to enjoy its natural wonders.

Minimizing Your Carbon Footprint

Choose Sustainable Transportation Options
Opt for sustainable transportation options when exploring Queenstown and the surrounding areas. Consider walking, cycling, or using public transportation whenever possible to minimize your carbon footprint. Queenstown offers a variety of eco-friendly transportation options, including electric bikes, hybrid buses, and walking trails that connect key attractions and destinations. Additionally, carpooling or ridesharing with other travellers can help reduce emissions and congestion on the roads.

Offset Your Carbon Emissions
Consider offsetting your carbon emissions by investing in carbon offset projects that support renewable energy, reforestation, and sustainable development initiatives. Many airlines and travel companies offer carbon offset programs that allow travellers to calculate their carbon footprint and contribute to projects that mitigate their environmental impact. By offsetting your carbon emissions, you can help support initiatives that combat climate change and promote sustainability on a global scale.

By adopting sustainable travel practices, such as choosing eco-friendly accommodations, practising responsible wildlife viewing, and minimizing your carbon footprint, you can make a positive impact on the environment and local communities during your visit to Queenstown. By embracing sustainable travel, you can help preserve the region's natural beauty, protect its wildlife and ecosystems, and support the livelihoods of residents. Together, we can ensure that Queenstown remains a vibrant and sustainable destination for generations to come, allowing travellers to continue to explore and appreciate its awe-inspiring landscapes and cultural heritage for years to come.

Chapter 18. Your Ultimate Guide to Travel Resources in Queenstown

Planning a trip to Queenstown? Whether you're a first-time visitor or a seasoned traveller, having access to the right travel resources can make all the difference in ensuring a smooth and enjoyable experience. From useful apps and websites to maps and guides, as well as insights into local customs and etiquette, here's everything you need to know to navigate your journey through Queenstown with ease.

Useful Apps and Websites

Queenstown NZ App

The Queenstown NZ App is your ultimate travel companion, offering a wealth of information and resources to help you make the most of your visit to Queenstown. From discovering top attractions and activities to finding restaurants, accommodations, and local services, this comprehensive app provides everything you need to plan your itinerary and navigate the town with ease. You can also access real-time updates on weather, events, and transportation, ensuring that you stay informed and prepared throughout your stay.

TripAdvisor

TripAdvisor is a valuable resource for travellers seeking reviews, recommendations, and insider tips on attractions, accommodations, restaurants, and more. Browse through user-generated reviews and ratings to discover hidden gems, popular hotspots, and must-visit destinations in Queenstown. Whether you're looking for adrenaline-pumping adventures, scenic hikes, or gourmet dining experiences, TripAdvisor can help you plan your itinerary and make informed decisions during your stay.

Maps and Guides

Official Queenstown Visitor Guide
Pick up a copy of the official Queenstown Visitor Guide upon arrival or download it online for easy access to essential information and resources. This comprehensive guide provides insights into top attractions, activities, accommodations, dining options, and local services in Queenstown and the surrounding areas. With detailed maps, itineraries, and insider tips from local experts, the Visitor Guide is your go-to resource for planning your adventure and exploring the best of Queenstown.

Google Maps
Google Maps is an invaluable tool for navigating the streets of Queenstown and finding your way around town. Use the app to access detailed maps, directions, and real-time traffic updates, ensuring that you reach your destination efficiently and without hassle. You can also use Google Maps to discover nearby attractions, restaurants, and points of interest, as well as locate public transportation options and walking routes to explore the town on foot.

Local Customs and Etiquette

Respect for Maori Culture

New Zealand has a rich indigenous heritage, and Maori culture plays an integral role in the country's identity and history. When visiting Queenstown and other parts of New Zealand, show respect for Maori customs, traditions, and protocols. Take the time to learn about Maori culture and history, and be mindful of cultural sensitivities when interacting with Indigenous communities or participating in cultural activities.

Environmental Conservation

Queenstown is known for its stunning natural beauty, and environmental conservation is a top priority for residents and visitors alike. Practice responsible tourism by minimizing your environmental impact, respecting wildlife and ecosystems, and following Leave No Trace principles when exploring nature. Dispose of waste properly, conserve water and energy, and support eco-friendly businesses and initiatives that prioritize sustainability and conservation.

With the right travel resources at your fingertips, navigating your journey through Queenstown becomes a seamless and enjoyable experience. From useful apps and websites to maps and guides, as well as insights into local customs and etiquette, you have everything you need to plan your adventure, explore the town, and immerse yourself in the beauty and culture of Queenstown. So pack your bags, download your apps, and get ready for an unforgettable journey through the breathtaking landscapes and vibrant communities of Queenstown, New Zealand.

Chapter 19. Appendices: Your Essential Reference Guide for Queenstown

In the bustling hub of Queenstown, it's essential to have quick access to important information and resources to ensure a safe and enjoyable visit. This appendix serves as your go-to reference guide, providing emergency numbers, a glossary of terms, and an index to help you navigate your journey through Queenstown with confidence and ease.

Emergency Numbers

Police: 111
In case of emergencies, including accidents, crimes, or incidents requiring immediate assistance from law enforcement, dial 111 to reach the New Zealand Police. Dispatchers are available 24/7 to respond to emergencies and dispatch officers to the scene as needed. When calling 111, provide clear details about the nature of the emergency and your location to facilitate a swift response.

Ambulance / Medical Emergency: 111
For medical emergencies, including injuries, illnesses, or medical crises, dial 111 to request ambulance services. Trained paramedics and emergency medical technicians are available to provide urgent medical care and transport patients to the nearest medical facility for further treatment. Be prepared to provide information about the patient's condition and location when calling 111 for medical assistance.

Fire and Rescue: 111
In the event of a fire or other emergencies requiring assistance from the fire department, dial 111 to reach Fire and Emergency New Zealand. Firefighters are trained to respond

to a wide range of emergencies, including fires, hazardous materials incidents, and vehicle accidents. Provide accurate information about the location and nature of the emergency when calling 111 for fire and rescue services.

Glossary of Terms

Kiwi:
A colloquial term used to refer to New Zealanders and the iconic flightless bird native to New Zealand.

Haka:
A traditional Maori dance or war cry is characterized by rhythmic movements, stamping, and chanting. The haka holds cultural significance and is often performed at ceremonial events, sports matches, and cultural celebrations.

Tiki Tour:
A leisurely drive or journey taken for pleasure or exploration, often with no particular destination in mind. The term "tiki tour" is derived from the Tiki, a Maori symbol representing fertility, and reflects the leisurely and meandering nature of the journey.

Index

A

- Accommodation: See Eco-Friendly Accommodations, Luxury Hotels, Budget-Friendly Options, Family-Friendly Stays, Unique Accommodations
- Adventure Sports: See Skydiving, White-Water Rafting, Mountain Biking, Ziplining
- Ambulance: See Emergency Numbers

E

- Eco-Friendly Accommodation: See Accommodation
- Emergency Numbers: See Police, Ambulance, Fire and Rescue

G

- Glossary of Terms: See Kiwi, Haka, Tiki Tour

I

- Index: See A, E, G

K

- Kiwi: See Glossary of Terms

P

- Police: See Emergency Numbers

T

- Tiki Tour: See Glossary of Terms

With the emergency numbers, glossary of terms, and index provided in this appendix, you have access to essential information and resources to navigate your journey through Queenstown with confidence and ease. Whether you need to contact emergency services, understand local terminology, or quickly find information in the index, this reference guide is your indispensable companion for a safe and enjoyable visit to Queenstown. So keep this guide handy during your travels, and embark on your adventure through the stunning landscapes and vibrant culture of Queenstown, New Zealand, with peace of mind and preparedness.

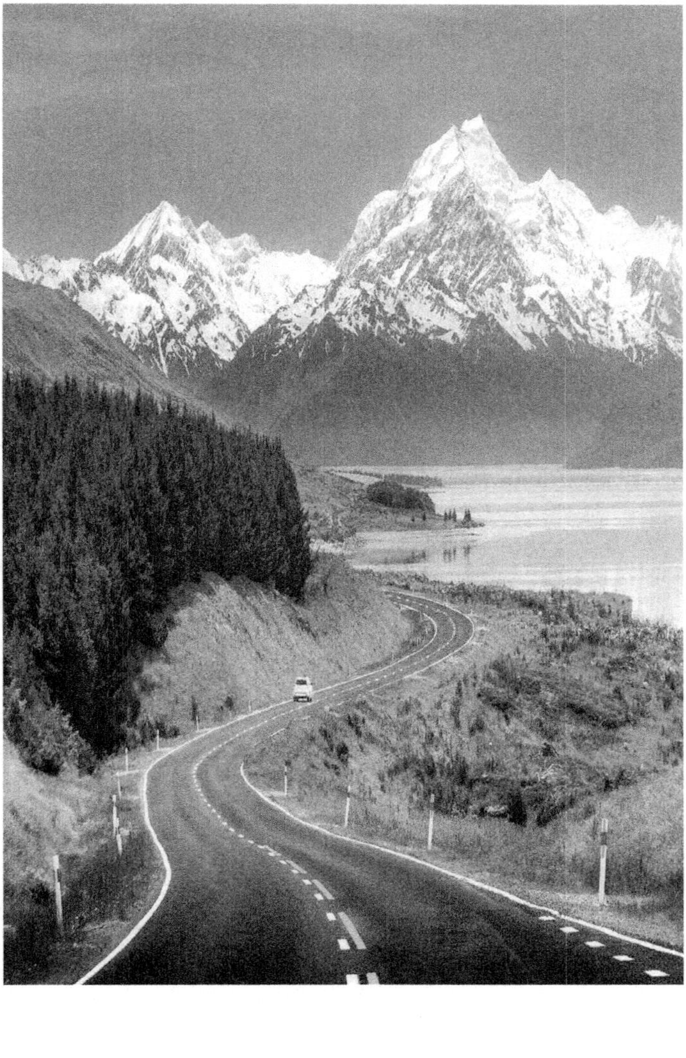

Printed in Great Britain
by Amazon